Top ICE HOCKEY Tips

BY HEATHER E. SCHWARTZ

Consultant: Mike Carroll
Head Women's Hockey Coach, Gustavus Adolphus College
St. Peter, Minnesota

CAPSTONE PRESS
a capstone imprint

Snap Books are published by Capstone Press
1710 Roe Crest Drive, North Mankato, Minnesota 56003
www.mycapstone.com

Library of Congress Cataloging-in-Publication Data is available on the Library of Congress website.

ISBN 978-1-5157-4723-9 (library hardcover)
ISBN 978-1-5157-4729-1 (paperback)
ISBN 978-1-5157-4747-5 (eBook PDF)

Summary: Learn the basics and the tips to playing ice hockey.

EDITORIAL CREDITS

Editor: Gena Chester
Designer: Veronica Scott
Media Researcher: Eric Gohl
Production Specialist: Kathy McColley

PHOTO CREDITS

Capstone Studio: Karon Dubke, 11, 13, 17; Getty Images: Boston Globe, 4–5, Portland Press Herald, 19, 21, 22 (bottom), 25, 29; Newscom/ZUMA Press: Brian Peterson, 6, 26, Bruce Bisping, 23, Eric Engman, 16, Kyndell Harkness, 24, Marlin Levison, 28; Shutterstock: Click Images, 10, darikuss, cover (net), Iurii Osadchi, 7, LifetimeStock, 12 (top), Lilyana Vynogradova, 15, 20 (bottom), Lorraine Swanson, 8 (bottom), Natan86, cover (puck & stick), 1, 8 (top), 12 (bottom), 18, 20 (top), 22 (top), 27, 32, Opka, 9, Shooter Bob Square Lenses (ice rink background)

Printed and bound in Canada
10040S17FR

TABLE OF CONTENTS

Face-Off!

Your heart pounds as you hold your stick poised and ready. Two players, one from each team, stand on the ice ready for the **face-off**. An official drops the puck between them. They battle for possession of the puck, and your teammate wins it! Her stick connects with the puck and sends it forward, toward you and the opposing team's net. Your **adrenaline** pumps as you skate after it, hoping to pass the puck to another teammate—or maybe even score yourself.

As an ice hockey player, you know the thrill of the game is about much more than winning. Each time you're on the ice, you test the skills you've developed for your sport and your position. You're challenged to work not only as an individual but also as a team player.

When you're not in a game, you spend time doing drills and going to practice. You know you can help your entire team as a stronger player.

face-off—a method of starting an ice hockey game by which an official drops the puck between two players

adrenaline—a hormone that causes increases in heart rate, pulse rate, and breathing rate

Chapter 1

THE *Basics*

Hockey is all about racking up points on the ice. It's a simple concept. But scoring goals on the opposing team is not nearly as simple as it sounds. Players from both teams try to gain control of the puck. They try to move it closer to the opposing team's net. At the same time, they need to keep it away from their own team's net. They shoot to score while opponents play defense and block the shots.

Each shot that makes it into the net earns one point for the team that scored. The team with the most points at the end of the game wins. Scoring isn't easy. At the highest levels in the sport, teams often score fewer than five points.

HOCKEY *History*

Much of ice hockey's history took place in Canada. In 1875, James Creighton organized the first ice hockey game in Nova Scotia, Canada. McGill University Hockey Club was the first recognized men's team. It started in 1880. The sport's popularity quickly spread throughout Canada. In 1892, the Montreal Amateur Athletic Association won the first Stanley Cup.

Women's ice hockey took a bit longer to get started. In 1889 Canadian Lord Preston flooded the front lawn of the Government House in Ottawa. When it froze, he and his sons and daughters used it to play hockey. This was the first documented account of girls playing ice hockey. By the 1920s, colleges in the United States and Canada had women's hockey teams. In 1990 Canada held the first Women's World Ice Hockey Championships. In 1998, women's ice hockey became an Olympic sport.

Leagues and Levels

Looking to join an ice hockey league? Some American high schools, mainly in Massachusetts and Minnesota, have girls' ice hockey teams. If you want to make the team, you'll need to attend tryouts first. At tryouts, the coach might have you show your skills in your preferred position, as well as other positions that could help the team.

You could also join a team through USA Hockey, an organization that oversees hockey in the United States. It puts youth players on teams according to age and skill. If players are good enough, they can move up to the next highest age bracket.

At the highest level, women can aim to play professionally for the National Women's Hockey League (NWHL). They can also aim to be a player in the Olympic Games.

Positions

Members of a team don't all play at once. Each team puts five skaters and one goalie on the ice. The coach calls players on and off the ice to make substitutions during the game. There is no pause in play while players enter and exit the game.

Positions that focus mainly on offense include the center, left wing, and right wing. These positions are also called forwards. They pass the puck to each other and try to score. They work on defense and try to block the opposing team's forwards.

Other skating positions include a left defenseman and a right defenseman. They focus on defense and keeping the puck out of their goal.

Goalies have one main focus. They block the puck from reaching the net. All players except the goalie skate up and down the rink. But goalies still need strong skating skills to quickly position themselves around the net to block shots. Any position—even the goalie—can shoot to score on the opposing team.

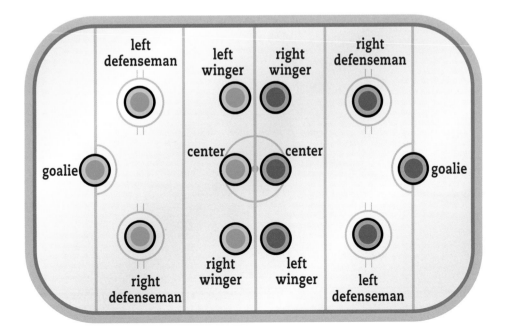

Chapter 2

SHARPEN YOUR

Skating Skills

The more skate time you can get, the more you can improve in hockey. When the puck travels in different directions during a game, it's your job to follow it. That means you need to be able to make quick movements on the ice—without falling down. Strong skating skills come in handy for puck handling, passing, and shots on goal. You can build those skills with balance drills.

Practice squats on the ice to improve balance. Glide forward on your skates. Squat as low as you can and keep gliding. Once that feels comfortable, incorporate a technique called "shoot the duck." Glide forward on one skate. Squat as low as you can while pushing the other leg straight out in front. Switch legs and repeat.

FIT TO *Skate*

The right skates are crucial to a hockey player's success on the ice. The skates must be fit to the individual player. Hockey skates are fit according to more than just skate size, width, and arch. The player's weight and skating ability are also factored in for the best possible fit.

~ *Tip* ~

Practice using your blade edges for better balance and control on your skates. Use your inside edges to push off the ice and accelerate as you skate. Use the inside edge on one foot and the outside edge on the other for turning and stopping.

Gain Speed

Speed on skates is important in hockey. Players have to chase the puck no matter where it winds up on the ice. Faster players have the best chance of reaching the puck first, so they can control where it goes next.

Hockey players can get faster on the ice by improving their speed off the ice. Most of the time, hockey players need to be fast for only short distances. Some drills and exercises are designed to make players faster in quick bursts.

Sprint the Distance

Mark a distance of 10 to 15 yards. Sprint as fast as you can while timing yourself. Take a rest break of about one minute, or long enough so you are breathing normally again. When you're fully recovered, sprint back. Do five sprints in a row. Try to improve your time each week.

Wall Sits

Wall sits can help you build your **gluteals** and **hamstrings** . This exercise is done off the ice. Press your back against a wall. Slide into a squat with your thighs parallel to the floor. Tighten your gluteals and hamstrings to make them do the work. Hold the position for 20 to 60 seconds. Repeat two more times with 30 second rest breaks in between. Make sure you have proper form! Your hands should be resting at your side or held out in front of you, not pressed into your legs or knees. Your knees should be directly above your ankles, not your toes.

gluteal—a muscle in the buttocks

hamstring—a tendon behind the knee

Skate Better Backward

Ice hockey players know it's not enough to have the skill to skate forward during a game. They also have to master skating backward. When players can skate easily both forward and backward, they can change direction quickly without losing control. They can keep their eyes on the action no matter where they need to move.

Build backward skating skills with backward swizzles. While skating backward it's important to keep your skates shoulder-width apart for balance. Bend your knees and press on the inside edges of your skate blades to glide backward.

Try back half swizzles to strengthen your skills. Point your right toe in and keep your left foot straight. Bend knees and press on the inside edge of your right skate blade to glide backward. Switch feet and repeat to continue moving backward.

~ *Tip* ~

You'll have better balance while skating backward (and forward) if your center of gravity is low to the ground. Keep your legs bent, back straight, and head up.

Chapter 3

STICK *Handling*

Stick-handling skills are crucial to any ice hockey player's success in the game. The more control you have over the puck, the more likely you'll score.

Strong **hand-eye coordination** helps hockey players develop their stick-handling skills. They can work their hand-eye coordination all year long with drills both on the ice and off.

hand-eye coordination—the ability to do things that involve your hands and eyes working together.

Grab your hockey stick and a small ball. Raise your stick parallel to the ground and hit the ball up in the air with the blade. Hit it over and over, keeping count until you drop it. When you try again, aim to beat your record. Use both sides of the stick blade during this drill to make it even more challenging.

Use your stick, a small ball, and a bucket for another kind of drill. Move the ball back and forth with your stick a few times. Then, scoop it up with your stick blade and deposit it in the bucket. Take it out and try it again to practice your **hand-eye coordination** and control.

SELECT THE RIGHT *Stick*

It's very hard for a hockey player to perform well without the right stick. Blade lie, curve, length, and flex can all help determine whether a stick is the best fit for an individual player.

BLADE LIE: the angle between the blade and the **shaft**. The blade angle allows the player to keep the stick's entire blade on the ice.

CURVE: describes how the blade is curved. Blades curve differently for right-handed and left-handed players.

LENGTH: based on the height of the player. With skates on, some players like it to reach the top of the nose. Others prefer it to reach their chin.

FLEX: refers to the stick's flexibility. Younger players usually use more flexible sticks. This allows them to feel the puck when passing and shooting.

shaft—the long handle of a hockey stick

Watch Where You're Going

Trying to connect your stick with the puck? Looking down at the puck might seem to make sense. But it's actually too limiting. When you're gazing at the ice, you can't see players coming at you. You also waste valuable time looking up and down, instead of planning where to skate next.

When hockey players learn good stick handling, they can control the puck without looking down all the time. They feel the puck through vibrations in their stick. With practice, the stick starts to feel like an extension of a player's arm. Players can learn puck control by dribbling.

Start on the ice with your head up with your stick in front of you and the puck in front of your stick blade. Move the puck forward by tapping it gently with the stick blade. Keep your head up as you continue tapping it forward, and skate to stay with it. Stay in control of the puck as you move to the other end of the ice.

~ *Tip* ~

Your feet can help
you handle the puck.
Practice using the blade
of your skate to stop the
puck and guide it to your
stick blade.

Chapter 4

PASS THAT *Puck*

Hockey players know teamwork is the key to scoring. Passing the puck gives you a chance to put the puck near the goal. It's the best way to help a teammate score. Passes are also the fastest way to get the puck away from your team's net.

There are many different kinds of passes hockey players can use during a game. The forehand pass uses the front of the blade to send the puck sliding on the ice. The backhand pass does the same, using the back side of the blade. The flip pass sends the puck up into the air. The saucer pass sends the puck sliding forward, jumping off the ice in a straight line.

Choosing which pass to use depends on the distance to your teammate, whether opposing players are in between, and other factors. The saucer pass, for example, is used to move the puck over obstacles, like the other team's sticks. The forehand and backhand pass work best when there aren't obstacles in the way.

~ Tip ~

Passing requires accuracy and aim. When you aim a pass for a teammate, your target is in motion. Aim ahead of the other player, so she will be able to meet the pass.

Pack the Power

Passing and shooting are most effective when hockey players combine accuracy with power. Ice hockey players skate forward as they pass. Their **momentum** creates power behind a shot. A powerful pass has a better chance of reaching a faraway target than a weak one. It's also harder for an opposing player to intercept.

Passing Practice

Practice transferring your weight as you move. Bend your knees to get leg muscles into the action. Notice how you transfer weight from your back leg to your front leg as you skate forward. The transfer should be made just as you connect your stick with the puck. Once this feels comfortable, step up your game. Grab a partner and practice passing back and forth as you skate down the length of the rink.

~ Tip ~

Build muscle in the weight room. Work muscles in your wrists, forearms, and legs to add power to your shots.

momentum—the strength or force something has while it is moving

Catch the Pass

Receiving the puck takes skill too. A pass that isn't received might wind up with the opposing team. Turn the blade of your stick down slightly toward the ice when receiving. This creates a pocket for the puck to land inside. Otherwise, the puck will bounce off and away.

Having soft hands helps hockey players receive the puck. When players have soft hands, it means they can react quickly to adapt their grip and stick position. This way the player absorbs the speed of the puck in the best way possible to catch the ball. For example, if a pass is coming in fast, she'll need to press the stick blade firmly on the ice.

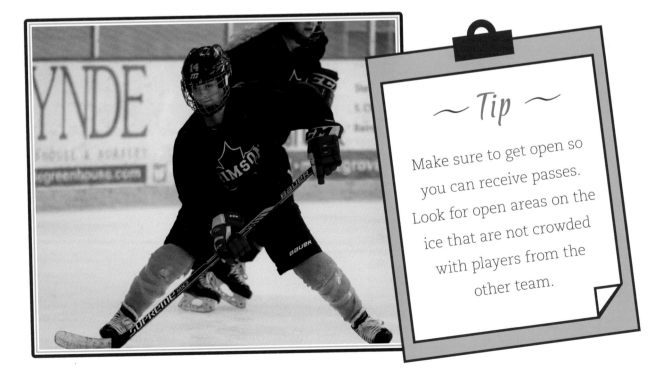

~ Tip ~

Make sure to get open so you can receive passes. Look for open areas on the ice that are not crowded with players from the other team.

Narrow Puck Drill

Grab a partner and practice precise passing. Skate forward with the puck, pushing it back and forth to your partner. Keep your passing controlled and catch the puck within the width of your shoulders.

Yard Sale

This drill helps you learn how to pass around obstacles to get the puck to your partner. Find several objects you can use as obstacles, such as cones, shoes, and gloves. Place them randomly in a small section of the ice. Handle the puck with your stick through and around the items to pass to your partner.

Chapter 5

SHOOT
to Score

When hockey players get a chance to score, they have to react fast. The wrist shot is a quick motion that draws power and precision from the wrist and forearm.

The wrist shot starts with the puck in front of the player. The player pulls the puck to her back leg. She cups the puck with her stick blade. To start the shot, she uses the blade to push the puck forward. Then, she lifts the blade and snaps down to lift the puck off the ice as she shoots. The wrist shot isn't easy to master. To pull it off successfully, a player must control where the puck goes both horizontally and vertically, so it will hit a top corner of the net. Practice is the best way to get better.

Line It Up!

Improve your wrist shot by taking three shots in a row for this drill. Line up three pucks on the blue line in front of the net. Choose one puck, skate toward the net, and shoot without stopping. Continue skating around the back of the net to get a second puck. Repeat until you've taken shots with all three pucks.

~ Tip ~

The puck won't always be perfectly positioned for you to make a shot. It's important to practice shooting with the puck in front of you, to the side of you, and even behind you.

ON THE *Ice*

In September 2011, 40 female ice hockey players started a high-scoring game that wouldn't end for many hours. The game in Burnaby, British Columbia, Canada, lasted 243 hours and five minutes to be exact. That's right—the players spent a total of 10 days on the ice! They played in four-hour shifts.

The final score reflected the lengthy game. Team White defeated Team Red 1372 to 978. Almost 2,500 goals were scored. But the players were more interested in other victories. The game raised $125,000 for cystic fibrosis. And it set a new world record for longest ice hockey game.

Score with the Slapshot

What's the hardest, fastest shot on goal in ice hockey? That would be the slapshot. The player raises her stick blade. Then, she slams it down to smack the puck with power. Megan Bozek, a professional player for the Buffalo Beauts, set the record for hardest shot in 2016. Her slapshot was 88 miles (141 kilometers) per hour. But the slapshot isn't just about force. It's about accuracy, too.

Practice Makes Perfect

Practice shooting high. Position yourself with your stick and puck in front of the net. Take high shots by keeping the blade open after it hits the puck. Aim the blade at a high spot on the net. Continue for about five minutes.

Aim low, too. If you can hit the bottom of the net with accuracy as well as the top, you'll have more chances to score. Position yourself with your stick and puck in front of the net. Hit the puck and follow through by rolling the stick blade over. Roll your wrists over sooner to keep the shot lower. Continue for about five minutes.

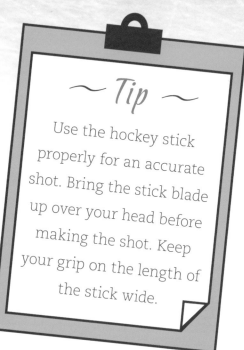

~ Tip ~

Use the hockey stick properly for an accurate shot. Bring the stick blade up over your head before making the shot. Keep your grip on the length of the stick wide.

From beginners to professionals, all ice hockey players work hard to improve their skills. If you love the game, you know the hard work is worth it. Every time you practice, prove you're up for a challenge. Do what it takes to become an impressive athlete on the ice.

GLOSSARY

adrenaline (uh-DREH-nuh-luhn)—a hormone that causes increases in heart rate, pulse rate, and breathing rate

face-off (FAYSS-awf)—a method of starting an ice hockey game by which an official drops the puck between two players

gluteal (gloo-TEE-uhl)—a muscle in the buttocks

hamstring (HAM-string)—a tendon behind the knee

hand-eye coordination (hand-EYE koh-OR-duh-nay-shun)—the ability to do things that involve your hands and eyes working together.

momentum (moh-MEN-tuhm)—the strength or force something has while it is moving

shaft (SHAFT)—the long handle of a hockey stick

toe pick (TOH PIK)—a section of jagged teeth at the front of a skate blade, which allows skaters to grip the ice better during jumps

READ MORE

Frederick, Shane. *The Ultimate Collection of Pro Hockey Records.* For the Record. North Mankato, Minn.: Capstone Press, 2013.

Hurley, Michael. *Ice Hockey.* Fantastic Sports Facts. North Mankato, Minn.: Capstone Press, 2013.

Labrecque, Ellen. *The Science of a Slap Shot.* Full-Speed Sports. Ann Arbor, Mich.: Cherry Lake Publishing, 2016.

INTERNET SITES

FactHound offers a safe, fun way to find Internet sites related to this book. All of the sites on FactHound have been researched by our staff.

Here's all you do:
Visit *www.facthound.com*

Type in this code: **9781515747239**

 Check out projects, games and lots more at
www.capstonekids.com

INDEX